WHEN EUROPE WENT MAD

A Brief History of the First World War

WHEN EUROPE WENT MAD

A Brief History of the First World War

TERENCE T. FINN

www.ivyhousebooks.com

PUBLISHED BY IVY HOUSE PUBLISHING GROUP
5122 Bur Oak Circle, Raleigh, NC 27612
United States of America
919-782-0281
www.ivyhousebooks.com

ISBN13: 978-1-57197-497-6
Library of Congress Control Number: 2009928283

Printed in the United States of America

To the memory of the American Expeditionary Force

- *Those who served*
- *Those who fought*
- *Those who died*

ACKNOWLEDGMENTS

In producing this book, I relied upon the scholarship of such eminent historians as John Keegan, Michael Neiberg, Hew Strachan, and H. P. Willmott as well as several others.

A list of these individuals and their work is provided at the end of the book. All are recommended.

Several people helped in the preparation of this book. Stephen Chitwood and Frederick Morhart reviewed the manuscript and made numerous suggestions all of which improved the text. Stace Wright contributed the two very useful maps. Tim Kenney skillfully designed the striking dust jacket. Mark Gillespie kindly wrote the Foreword. I'm grateful to all five gentlemen, and to Marla Handelmann, who lent her professional talents to the project. I'm grateful, too, to Joyce Purcell who, as always, provided encouragement and her finely tuned editorial skills. Any errors, of course, are mine alone.

Mention also must be made of the contributions by the staff at Ivy House Publishing Group, specifically Anna Howland, Tami Stoy, and Ashley Hardin. My thanks to them all.

—TERENCE T. FINN

PROLOGUE

This book looks at one of the major military conflicts of all time, one in which the United States played a small but significant role. It provides a brief account of the First World War, explaining why the United States went to war and how the war was fought. It tells the story of the entire conflict describing the fifty-one months of bloodshed as the nations of Europe took up arms in 1914, eventually causing the death of some fifteen million people. Purposefully, the narrative in this book is short although it attempts to go beyond the recitation of facts and dates to capture the spirit of the times.

The book previews a larger, future work in which all the wars America has fought are similarly described. This later book will start with the War for Independence and, with each chapter devoted to a major conflict, will take the reader up to the present.

When Europe Went Mad targets readers whose familiarity with history is limited, but who are curious and wish to learn more about World War One and the part America played in it. These individuals are not looking for a treatise or complex analysis. They just want to know what happened and what was important. They seek a readable, narrative account that, while short in length, is complete and informative. This book attempts to provide both.

—TERENCE T. FINN

FOREWORD

Although some historians have referred to previous conflicts such as The Seven Years War of 1756-1763 as the first world war, no conflict prior to that of 1914-1918 affected so many of the world's principal nations across multiple continents and several years. As a brief account of the First World War, Terence Finn's book concisely introduces readers to this conflagration, one that forever changed the balance of world power and presaged the even more destructive global conflict of World War Two.

Prior to 1914, the European Great Powers of England, France, Germany, Italy, and Russia, taken together, had achieved the feat of conquering vast territories throughout the world and dividing them up into their colonial empires. This process began several centuries earlier with conquests by Spain, Portugal, and the Netherlands. These early European colonial powers eventually declined and were overtaken by the European Great Powers that clashed in the First World War. This struggle for colonial possessions reached its zenith just prior to the outbreak of war in 1914 with England, France, and Germany harnessing the enormous power of their industrial revolutions and channeling it into the production of powerful navies backed up with modern land forces capable of subduing nearly any non-industrialized nation.

As the competition for securing colonial territories escalated principally between Great Britain and Germany, the friction generated gave rise to increasing diplomatic tensions within Europe. As a result of these tensions plus other factors best examined in a more comprehensive treatment of the time period, two opposing alliance systems formed that set the parameters for the looming conflict. The Triple Alliance had formed earlier in 1882 consisting originally of Germany, Austro-Hungary and Italy as a bonding of central European countries. By 1907, understandings among the former colonial archrivals England, France and Russia created the opposing Triple Entente. A series of crises beginning in Morocco in 1905 and extending to the Balkans, culminating in the assassination of the Austro-Hungarian Archduke Ferdinand, provided a final spark that set off the explosive mixture that engulfed the world in conflict. When the conflict actually came in 1914 Italy declared neutrality and, after obtaining assurances of territorial rewards for doing so, joined the Triple Entente in 1915 in active combat against Germany, Austro-Hungary and Germany's new ally as of August 1914, the Ottoman Empire.

The First World War saw the splintering and destruction of global domination by the European powers making way for the rise of new great powers from America and Japan. The results of the First World War were staggering in terms of the magnitude of the destruction wrought and the shattering of great powers such as the Austro-Hungarian and the Ottoman empires, with the latter's demise still having repercussions on the course of history in the Middle East today. Although among the ultimate victors in the war, England and France emerged considerably battered and diminished in power. They nonetheless proceeded to carve up the Middle Eastern territories of the toppled Ottoman Empire and brought them into their respective colonial empires. To contemporary native observers in colonial lands at the time, as well as from the perspective of today, it seemed the Europeans had in 1914 truly gone mad.

This book also provides a useful initial look at the type of warfare encountered in the First World War. The opposing forces of the world's Great Powers collided on a global scale in fierce combat for the first time in all three dimensions of land, sea, and air, thus providing an initial glimpse at the horrors unleashed by modern technology. Engaging in total warfare, these nations inflicted great harm on both civilians and military personnel alike. Moreover, war forced mobilization of practically all the resources of the countries involved, including women who served actively in supporting roles at home and on the battlefront.

At sea submarines employed by the Germans engaged in unrestricted warfare that provided their targets no prior warning of attack. As Dr. Finn's book correctly reveals, this was a tactic viewed by many in the United States and elsewhere as totally uncivilized. In the air, German bombers in the form of Zeppelin airships dropped bombs on population centers such as London. This was seen by many as equally uncivilized. In addition, the Germans began using poisonous gas to attack their foes in 1915, escalating from non-lethal tear gas that had been used by both sides prior to that time. Although both sides soon routinely used various forms of poisonous gas against their enemies, the initial use by the Germans further condemned them as being beyond the bounds of civilized conduct in the eyes of many. This also left the Germans vulnerable to efforts conducted principally by the British to bring the United States into the war.

The author's narrative of the costly stalemate that evolved on the Western Front in the First World War also gives the reader an indication of the deadly results when advances in technology outstrip the application of tactics used by the commanding generals on both sides. Technological improvements in artillery enabled sustained massive barrages by rapid firing, long-range and highly accurate field pieces leading to a high probability that massed infantry attacks on foot in vogue at that time would fail. The industrial capacities of both sides to produce and deliver staggering amounts of artillery ammunition to the front combined with the liberal use of barbed-wire obstacles covered by rapid firing machine guns further contributed to the ability of defending forces to successfully halt offensive maneuvers. These technological factors also served to make horse cavalry tactics completely ineffective on the Western Front. The technological innovation of mechanized tanks first seen in September 1916 by the British caused a very limited reintroduction of mobility to the stalemate on the Western Front, but their tactical use by war's end in 1918 never lived up to their potential that would later be demonstrated by mechanized forces in the next world war that followed less than twenty-one years later.

The extensive scholarship that exists on the First World War provides considerable insight into the political, economic, financial, and military aspects of the great conflict. Although much of the work scholars have produced is worth examining, generally the length and level of detail are likely to be unsuitable for those readers who seek a brief but complete account of the war. For this purpose, Terence Finn's book serves admirably.

—MAJ. MARK GILLESPIE (USA, Ret.)

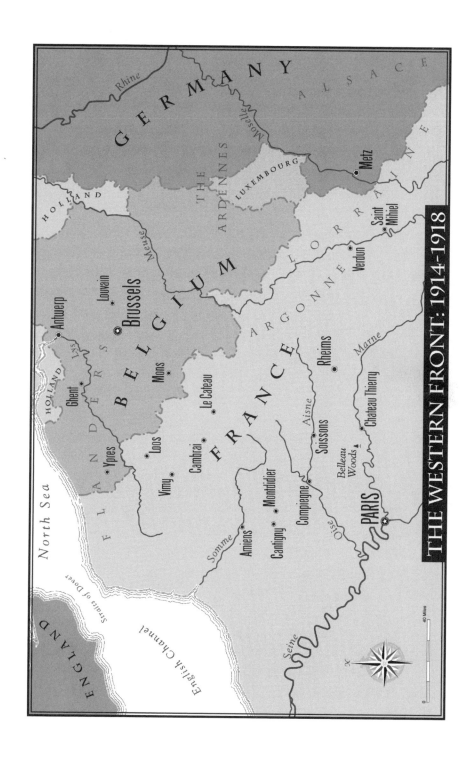

THE WESTERN FRONT: 1914-1918

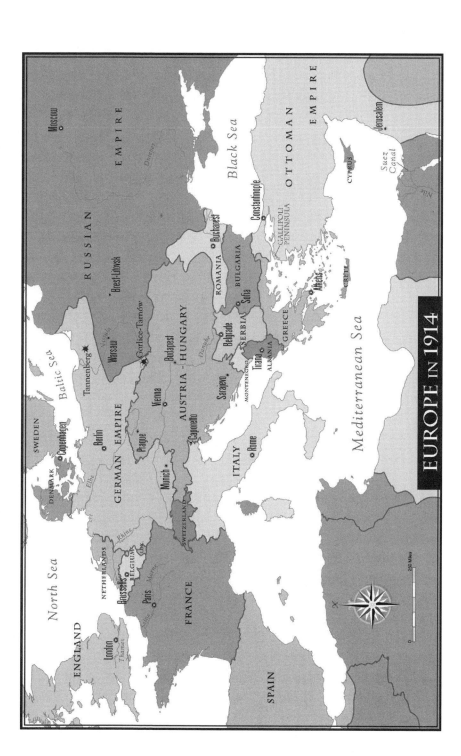

EUROPE IN 1914

WORLD WAR ONE

In June 1914, a single act of political murder in Bosnia set in motion a sequence of events that resulted in a war in Europe, a war that soon reached far distant parts of the globe. The impact of this conflict would be devastating to both individuals and nations. Over eight million soldiers would lose their lives. They would die in mud, in the desert, on snow-covered mountains, and at sea. They even would die in the air. In France, 630,000 women would become widows. In Belgium, Serbia, Turkey, and elsewhere, innocent civilians, including women and children, would perish, many of them simply executed. Countries too would die, and maps would need to be redrawn. The Austro-Hungarian Empire of the Hapsburgs would disappear. The German Imperial State would collapse and its Kaiser would move to Holland, emperor no longer. The Ottoman Empire, then ruler of what is now Turkey and much of the Middle East, would share the fate of the Hapsburgs and cease to exist. The Tsar and Romanoff rule in Russia would come to a violent end, replaced by the Bolsheviks. America, late to the war, would emerge relatively unscathed, in better shape than all the nations that earlier had sent their young men to fight and die.

The conflict of 1914-1918 was to be a milestone in human history. Nothing like it had ever occurred. Those who lived through it called it The Great War. Today, less aware of its impact, we refer to it simply as World War One.

ONE

Archduke Franz Ferdinand was the heir to the throne of the Austro-Hungarian Empire. This was an empire that had seen better days. Comprised of many different nationalities—its subjects spoke twelve different languages—the Austro-Hungarian state in 1914 was a ramshackle affair, conservative to the core, with an army that was large, but not terribly effective. On June 28, their wedding anniversary, Franz Ferdinand and his wife Sophie were in Sarajevo, the capital of Bosnia, which though part of the empire, contained many Serbs. To the south and adjacent to Bosnia was Serbia, an independent nation whose people then, as now, were prone to violence. The Serbs detested the Empire of Austria-Hungary whose rulers reciprocated the feeling.

Thus, no one was surprised when, with the complicity of Serbia, a young Bosnian radical shot and killed the Archduke and his wife. Correctly blaming Serbia, the Empire, with Germany's approval, declared war on its southern neighbor. That upset Russia which, because of race and religion, considered itself the protector of Serbia. Russia mobilized its armed forces. That, in turn, alarmed Germany, which saw Russia and its vast number of men eligible for military service as a direct threat to its security. Germany then put its armed forces on notice, which, in turn, made the French extremely nervous. Forty years earlier, France had been invaded by Germany and, defeated in battle, had ceded to the victor the eastern provinces of Alsace and Lorraine. These the French considered theirs and hoped some day to regain. When the German army mobilized, France naturally enough brought its own military to full alert.

★ ★ ★

In 1914, most military experts believed that the army that attacked first would win. Armies that found themselves on the defensive, these experts predicted, likely would lose. As soon as mobilization had been ordered, most generals, and certainly those of the Kaiser, believed the war in effect had begun. Once Russia had ordered its army to get ready, German generals considered their country at war.

Though formally at peace with one another, the nations comprising Europe in 1914 were highly distrustful of those countries they viewed as adversaries. Competing desires for empire, rivalry in trade and industry, different political traditions and forms of government, as well as armies and navies that planned for war all made Europe a tinderbox ready to explode. The assassination of Franz Ferdinand provided the spark. True, diplomacy could have doused the flame, but it did not. The result was that in August 1914, the world went to war, and the killing began.

Geography had not been kind to Germany. To its east lay Russia, to its west, France. With good reason, these countries viewed the Kaiser's army with alarm. They had an agreement that if one were attacked, the other would come to its aid. Hence, Germany found itself trapped. Each of the two, so the Kaiser believed, sought to deny Germany's rightful place in Europe and the world. But France and Russia were not the only nations serving to hold Germany back. With its huge navy, Great Britain also stood ready to limit Germany's influence. In response Imperial Germany, under the guidance of

Admiral Alfred von Tirpitz, had built a strong navy. It was not as powerful as Britain's, but it was a force sufficient to cause concern.

German war strategy in 1914 took into account both geography and the armed forces of Russia, France, and Britain. First developed by Alfred von Schlieffen, chief of the German General Staff from 1891 to 1905, its essence was retained by Helmuth von Moltke, who in 1914 was the German army's commander-in-chief. Moltke and Schlieffen reasoned that Russia could not mobilize its troops quickly. Germany's best bet then was to strike first at France and do so with overwhelming strength. The plan was to defeat Germany's enemy in the west then, by rail, transport the victorious army to the east to confront the Russians. The Kaiser's generals estimated they had 40 days to beat the French. After that, the Russian menace in the east had to be addressed. Moreover, given that Russia would grow stronger over time, it would be best to strike sooner rather than later.

France, too, had prepared for war. It had constructed a series of powerful forts along its border with Germany. Any attack there by the Kaiser's troops would run into interlocking fields of fire intended to halt the German advance. But General Joseph Joffre, chief of the French army, wanted to do more than simply hold back the Germans. He wanted his forces to attack. His plan, labeled War Plan XVII, envisioned an offensive into Germany the goal of which was to retake Alsace and Lorraine.

Aware of the forts and of France's desire to recover Alsace and Lorraine, Schlieffen had developed an extremely bold plan. The German army would strike not across the border with France. Rather, it would attack from the northwest, through Belgium. The army's right wing, its most powerful element, would swing wide, crushing both Belgian and French forces, then sweep south to the west of Paris coming around the city to hit from the rear those French forces that were facing the rest of the German attack.

Though aware that marching through Belgium might bring Great Britain into the war, Germany's generals were not concerned. The British army was small and not likely to arrive in time. And, if it did, it easily could be pushed aside. As for Belgium, its army, too, was small. The forts upon which it relied for defense simply were to be blown to pieces by specially designed heavy guns. Could Moltke and the eight separate field armies he had at his disposal execute von Schlieffen's plan?

★ ★ ★

On August 4, 1914, German forces crossed into Belgium heading for France. Two armies were kept home to protect Alsace and Lorraine. Another, the Eighth, was positioned to the east guarding the nation's border with Russia. Thus, Moltke dispatched five separate German armies to hit the French. Two of them, the First and the Second, constituted the strong right wing of the strike force. Commanded respectively by Generals Alexander von Kluck and Karl von Bulow, they together numbered well over half a million men. It was an impressive force. The Kaiser and his army commander-in-chief believed it was unstoppable.

It was true that Belgium's army was small, but when King Albert ordered it to oppose the Germans it did so, and it did so bravely. The results, however, were as the Kaiser's generals had predicted. The forts were destroyed and those Belgian soldiers not killed or wounded retreated, joining up with the French Fifth Army, which had responsibility for defending the far left flank of all French forces. In this, the Fifth Army failed, mauled by advancing German troops. Its commander soon would be sacked by Joffre. As the German onslaught continued and France's military fortunes declined, Joffre replaced more than a few senior officers he considered unequal to their jobs.

The French commander-in-chief, true to his desire for offensive action and consistent with War Plan XVII, had sent two armies into Alsace and Lorraine. Attacking along a 75-mile front, the soldiers ran into the two armies Moltke had deployed there. At first the French did well. But, by late August, they had given way in the face of strong German counterattacks. Casualties on both sides were heavy. One French division, numbering 15,000 troops, had 11,000 killed or wounded.

By this time the British too had suffered losses. Once Belgium's neutrality had been violated by the Germans, the government in London had sent most of the British army to France. What was called the British Expeditionary Force (BEF) began arriving on August 14. It went into action almost immediately. At Mons and Le Cateau, the soldiers of King George V fought hard, inflicted casualties upon the Germans, but fell back. At Le Cateau, a small village southeast of Cambrai, the BEF had 8,000 men killed or wounded. Not since Waterloo in 1815 had Britain's army seen such combat.

To this point the Germans had done quite well. They had pushed aside the Belgians, defeated the French, and caused the British to retreat. Closing in on Paris, they reached the Marne River on September 3. That same day the French government abandoned the capital setting up shop in Bordeaux, far to the south. Soon German troops crossed the Marne. Some of their heavy guns began shelling Paris. Victory for the Kaiser and his generals seemed close at hand.

However, Joseph Joffre did not panic. Calmly, as the Germans advanced, he redeployed his troops (as each day he calmly enjoyed a lengthy lunch then took a nice nap). He also took note of a gap that had opened between the German First and Second Armies. The former, Kluck's command, had not circled west of Paris. Intent on destroying French forces before him, he had swayed from Schlieffen's original plan. Paris was on his right flank. To his left, but not close by, was Bulow's Second Army.

All along a 200-mile front, the battled raged. Defending the French capital to Kluck's right was the French Sixth Army. Among its soldiers was the garrison of Paris. Its commander, General Joseph Gallieni, had requisitioned 600 Renault taxicabs to transport these troops, five men at a time, to the army. He soon would become known as "the savior of Paris." His vehicles, the taxis, would pass into legend.

Further to the east, very much in the fight, Joffre had placed the newly created Ninth Army. Its commander, Ferdinand Foch, had performed well in the defense of Nancy, a major city in northeastern France. In 1918, Foch would play a key role in the Allies' final victory. He was a capable commander with an aggressive approach to warfare. In the Battle of the Marne he drafted a signal that, like the Parisian taxis, would become legendary: "My center is giving way, my right is in retreat, situation excellent. I attack."[1]

The Kaiser's troops fought hard, but they had marched a long way since crossing into Belgium. They were tired and no longer at full strength having suffered numerous casualties. More importantly, by early September they were short of supplies. Logistics—that critical component of both ancient and modern warfare—were to be their undoing. Increasingly the German army could not keep its divisions fighting in France adequately supplied. German units were short of practically everything, particularly food. So, the Kaiser's generals were forced to concede failure. On September 9, the fortieth day, Bulow ordered his Second Army to withdraw. This meant the other German armies had to do the same. The Battle of the Marne was over.

Joffre had won. The "Miracle of the Marne" had saved France. Church bells rang and the nation celebrated. The cost had been high. In the month of September in the year 1914, the French army had sustained more than 200,000 casualties. October would see that number increase by 80,000. By the end of the year after but five months of war, 306,000 French soldiers were dead. Twice that many were wounded.

For Germany, the Marne represented its best chance to win the First World War. Unlike the successful campaign against France in 1870–71, the Kaiser's armies in 1914 did not crush their opponents nor cause a government to topple. Despite successes on individual battlefields the German efforts in Belgium and France fell short. Yet, though tired and short of supplies, by no means were the German armies a spent force. They retired in good order, retreating to high ground at the Aisne River. There, in addition to emplacing machine guns and siting artillery batteries, they began to dig. So did the French who pursued them. Soon, the trenches that so characterize The Great War laced the landscape. As winter set in, they would run a distance of 475 miles without a break, extending from the Swiss border to the North Sea.

Two

As a result of the German army's failure at the Marne, Helmuth von Moltke lost his job. His replacement as commander-in-chief was General Erich von Falkenhayn. By October, given the line of well-defended trenches, the only place where an army might outflank its opponent was to the northwest. Falkenhayn focused on a small spot in Belgium still held by the French and British. If he could have success there he would gain control of those ports nearest to England, thus making operations extremely difficult for the BEF, possibly compelling Great Britain to leave the war. Were that to happen he would be able to concentrate his armies in the west solely upon the French. Despite the outcome at the Marne, Falkenhayn saw in this approach an avenue to victory.

The fighting that resulted lasted for over five weeks. Falkenhayn's soldiers fought Belgian, French, and British troops. Collectively, the engagements are recorded as First Ypres after the medieval town in Belgium around which much of the fighting took place. This first clash was costly to all involved. Together, in excess of 200,000 men were either killed or wounded. In the end, the Germans failed to advance as Falkenhayn had hoped.

For the British, First Ypres would be a memorable battle. Not because they won, which they did, though with heavy casualties, but because it marked the passing of the small,

professional army Great Britain had established to fight its battles on land. By the end of 1914, most of the 100,000 men
who constituted that army were gone. Many were dead, many
were wounded. From 1915 on, the British army would have
to rely on volunteers and conscripts, young men with little
training whose military skills would take time to develop.

If First Ypres left a mark on the British—and it did—it
also left a mark as well upon the Germans. In pushing forward
on the attack, Falkenhayn's forces included a large number of
university students who eagerly had volunteered for the army.
Hastily, they were given uniforms and rifles and, with little
preparation, were rushed into battle. The results were catastrophic. Over 25,000 were killed. In Germany their deaths
became known as *Kindermord*, the Massacre of the Innocents.
John Keegan, a highly regarded military historian, notes in his
fine book on World War One that the insignia of every German university are displayed at the cemetery where the 25,000
are buried in a mass grave.[2]

Holding off the Germans at First Ypres meant that the
British and French retained control of a small slice of Belgium.
The rest of that country was occupied by the Kaiser's forces.
These troops, with the approval of senior army commanders,
acted with extreme cruelty toward Belgian civilians. They simply took many of them away and shot them. In addition, they
looted and wantonly burned buildings. This barbaric behavior
included the destruction of the ancient university town of
Louvain with its unique library that housed irreplaceable Medieval and Renaissance works of art. What became known as
"the Rape of Belgium" appalled thoughtful people throughout the world. It served to inflame British public opinion,
which helped sustain Britain's commitment to battle. It also

contributed to a belief in the United States that Germany did
not deserve to win the war.

Both Moltke and Falkenhayn had concentrated Germany's
forces in the west, hoping to defeat France before Russia was
capable of waging war. But the Tsar mobilized his troops more
quickly than expected. Two Russian armies soon attacked,
crossing into East Prussia in mid-August. Defending Germany
was a single army, the Eighth. Its commander was a retired soldier brought back to active duty, Count Paul von Hindenburg.
His chief of staff was General Erich Ludendorff. Together, they
made a formidable team. In late August 1914, they crushed
the Russians at Tannenberg. One of the Russian armies was
completely destroyed. Mortified by the totality of his defeat, its
commander wandered off into the woods and shot himself.
Casualties were high, but the most notable statistic is the number of Russians captured. At Tannenberg the German Eighth
Army took 90,000 prisoners! The battle was one of the great
engagements of the First World War. Germany's victory was
complete. Hindenburg became a national hero. Later on, when
Falkenhayn was dismissed, the Kaiser appointed Hindenburg
as the army's commander-in-chief. Ludendorff became chief
military planner. As the war progressed, Hindenburg became
more of a figurehead while Ludendorff decided where and
when German troops would fight.

For the next three years, 1915-1917, the Germans and
Russians would do battle. Most of the time, the Germans won.
In 1915, the Kaiser's generals scored a huge victory near the
towns of Tarnow and Gorlice in what is now Poland (at that
time there were Poles, but no independent nation of Poland,
as the territory was part of the Tsar's empire). What is remark-
able today is the scale of the battles. Thousands upon thousands
of men fought and died. In the campaign of Tarnow-Gorlice
the Russian army suffered nearly one million casualties. In
pushing the Russians out of Poland, the Germans took

750,000 prisoners. In 1916, in a rare Russian victory over both German and Austrian troops, General Alexi Brusilov's offensive inflicted 600,000 casualties upon the enemy. In the Caucasus, where the Ottoman and Russian empires collided, the Turks lost more than 60,000 men in an unsuccessful attack upon the Russians. Many of these soldiers died of frostbite as the Turkish commander unwisely chose to attack in December, when snow and bitter cold made maneuvers difficult.

Despite these successes, the war did not go well for Russia. Military defeat in the field and political unrest at home led to revolution. On March 15, 1917, the Tsar abdicated (and later was executed). The liberal Socialist Alexander Kerensky and his government were also toppled (although he was not killed). Lenin and the Bolsheviks took control and at once secured an armistice with Germany. The Kaiser and his generals were in no mood for leniency. At Brest-Litovsk they laid down harsh terms. The Russians had no choice but to accept. Huge amounts of once-Russian territories were transferred to German control, including what are now Poland, Ukraine, the Baltic states, and Finland. One-third of Russia's agricultural land was lost. Nine percent of its coal reserves were gone. The result of failure in battle, the Treaty of Brest-Litovsk humiliated Russia. Far more than territory had been sacrificed. By the end of 1917, nearly five million Russian soldiers had been wounded; one million, eight hundred thousand were dead.

As the Russians were crushed by the Germans, so too were the Romanians. In 1916, emboldened by General Brusilov's initial successes and hoping to gain additional territory once Germany was defeated, Romania went to war. Siding with Great Britain, France, and Russia (the Triple Entente), Romanian forces attacked west, advancing 50 miles into Transylvania, then an area belonging to the Austro-Hungarian Empire, but in which a large number of Romanians resided. Germany's response was prompt and forceful. One German army, which included troops from Bulgaria and Austria, crossed into Romania from the south along the coast. Another attacked from the north. Together they disposed of Romania's army as well as Russian regiments sent to help. Victorious, German infantry entered Bucharest, the capital of Romania, on December 6, 1916. An armistice soon followed, then a treaty of peace. As with Brest-Litvosk, the terms were harsh. Romania possessed four assets: oil, grain, railroads, and part of the Danube. The Germans took control of all four. Romania, in effect, became a vassal state. However, it would have the last laugh. At Versailles in 1919, in the treaties that formally concluded the First World War, Romania, having chosen the winning side, was rewarded with Transylvania. Even today the region constitutes the northern portion of the country.

THREE

Throughout World War One, Germany's principal allies were the Austro-Hungarian Empire and the Empire of the Ottomans. The latter was quite large, covering what is today Turkey, Iraq, Syria, Lebanon, Israel, Jordan, and parts of Saudi Arabia (Egypt and Kuwait were British protectorates). Because the empire was in decline, its army needed assistance. This the Germans provided. Indeed, during the last years of the war, the commander of most Turkish forces in Palestine was Erich von Falkenhayn. Among troops at his disposal were 18,000 German and Austrian soldiers. In 1916, General Falkenhayn had led one of the German armies in Romania. By 1917, he was in the Middle East. There he had less success. Earlier, British troops had repulsed a Turkish assault upon the Suez Canal and retaken Baghdad, a British garrison of 12,500 men near the city having surrendered in April 1916. In 1917, Falkenhayn's task was to hold on to Palestine. But in a series of engagements with the British, he was unable to do so. General Edmund Allenby defeated the Turks and their German commander and, on December 11, 1917 entered Jerusalem in triumph.

Of considerable assistance to Allenby was a large number of Arab warriors who had little love for their Turkish rulers. A British intelligence officer, T.E. Lawrence, helped convince them to aid Allenby. They did so, in part due to British promises of independence once the war ended. Of course, the British had no intention of honoring these promises as the Arabs discovered at Versailles.

Like the army of the Ottomans, the army of the Austro-Hungarian Empire required German assistance. The Hapsburg army was large and certainly not lacking in courage. But, in early battles with the Russians along their common border, the army was worn down. By the end of 1914, just months into the war, it had incurred 1,200,000 casualties. Twelve weeks into 1915 saw that number increase by 800,000. Many of these soldiers constituted the core capability of the army and could not be replaced. As the war continued their absence was felt. The Empire's army, while still large, was not effective. It needed help. This came from Germany in the form of men and supplies. In fact, German generals essentially took over command of their ally's army. More than one German commander said the Kaiser's army, to use the phrase highlighted by noted historian Hew Strachan, was "shackled to a corpse."[3]

If there was one nation upon which the Austro-Hungarian Empire wished to wreak havoc, it was Serbia. Since June 1914, revenge for the assassination of Franz Ferdinand was never far from the minds of the Hapsburg leaders. Very early in the war the Austro-Hungarians attacked. Remarkably, the Serbs held them off. Despite the setbacks and 227,000 casualties, the Austrians had no intention of quitting. They turned to the Germans and to the Bulgarians and, in the fall of 1915, troops from all three countries invaded Serbia. They were under the command of one of Germany's better generals, August von Mackensen. He had won the great victory at Tarnow and Gorlice, and in 1916 would lead one of the German armies into Romania. His efforts in 1915 soon had the Serbs in full retreat. The defenders fought hard, suffering 94,000 casualties. But, their opponent was too strong and Serbia's army and government had to flee. Their epic march across Montenegro and

Kosovo to the Adriatic Sea, where Allied ships took them off, is today part of Serbian legend.

The soldiers of Austria-Hungary fought not only the Serbs and the Russians, but also fought the Italians. Italy and the Austro-Hungarian Empire shared a 400-mile border. This was mostly mountains, which favored those waging a defensive battle. Nevertheless, and to their great credit, the Italians attacked, fighting along the Isonzo River (a river near the northeastern corner of the Italian Republic that flows into the Gulf of Trieste). Indeed, in the years 1914 through 1917, they attacked eleven times. For their efforts, however, they gained little ground while suffering substantial casualties. Here again, the scale of military operations in the First World War is evident. The total number of men wounded or killed in 1915 in combat between two second-tier states, Italy and Austria-Hungary, on a battlefront considered primary by neither the British, French, or German commanders was slightly over 424,000.

The number of casualties would increase. In the eleventh battle along the river in August 1917, the Italians suffered an additional 155,000. This time, they made significant gains, so much so that Austria-Hungary, alarmed, requested assistance from Germany.

Germany gathered together several infantry divisions and, with troops from the Austro-Hungarian Empire established a new army, the Fourteenth, which attacked the Italians in October 1917. In but a few weeks, the Fourteenth Army achieved a great victory, driving the Italians back a distance of some 60 miles. This, the Battle of Caporetto, remains a painful memory for Italy and its army. Ten thousand Italian soldiers were killed and three times that number were wounded. Almost unbelievably, and another indicator of the state of the 1914-1918 conflict, German troops took 275,000 Italians prisoner. Yet, the Italian army recovered. A year later, it went on the offensive, supported by British, French and American units. It fought well and across a wide front pushed the Austrians back. This success, achieved right at the end of the war, earned Italy a seat at the head table when at Versailles the Allies redrew the map of Europe. As did Romania, Italy came away with additional territory that remains part of the country today.

Serbia, Romania, the Italian Alps and the Caucasus, Bulgaria and Palestine, are all places far from the trenches of Western Europe. For most Americans, it is these trenches that have come to symbolize the First World War. Yet, in each location, just mentioned generals issued orders, soldiers obeyed, and men died. But there are two additional places that saw military operations during the Great War, places not usually associated with the conflict of 1914–1918. These are Africa and China. Both witnessed the clash of arms.

In 1914, Imperial Germany had an outpost on the northern coast of China, at Tsingtao. Eager to expand its influence and believing Germany to be otherwise occupied, Japan, with Britain's concurrence, landed 60,000 troops nearby and, in early November 1914, took control of the city. During the same period, Japan also seized German outposts on the Caroline and Marshall Islands. None of this came as a surprise to the generals and admirals in Berlin because Japan had declared war on Germany months before, on August 23.

In addition to outposts in China and the Pacific islands, Germany also had a presence in Africa. So did other European powers, most notably Britain, France and Belgium. Germany controlled what then was called Togoland, Kamerum, German South-West Africa and German East Africa and, what is today Togo, parts of Cameron, Ghana, Tanzania and Nambia. In all four locations, British and German forces went to war, with both sides employing mostly native soldiers (the French brought their African troops north and employed them in the trenches where, no doubt, the rain and cold came as quite a shock). Eventually, the British carried the day, although in German East Africa 100,000 British troops were unable to defeat decisively 15,000 irregulars of the enemy. The latter were led brilliantly by the German Paul von Lettow-Vorbeck who, both during and after the war, was a national hero.

FOUR

Lettow-Vorbeck never had to deal with trench warfare where barbed-wire, heavy artillery, aerial observation, and machine gun nests made both attacking and defending a hazardous occupation. Joffre and Falkenhayn did, as did Sir John French, the commander of the British Expeditionary Force. In 1915, all three generals went on the offensive. The result for each of them was failure. Their armies gained very little ground, but suffered substantial casualties.

The French in particular took heavy losses. In the autumn, attacks alone Joffre's army had 190,000 soldiers killed or wounded. At Loos, in September 1915, the BEF saw 16,000 of its men dead with another 25,000 wounded. Four months before, at the Second Battle of Ypres, a German assault also resulted in numerous casualties. The Germans, who again failed to push the British out of the city, suffered 38,000 dead or wounded. What makes Second Ypres singularly noteworthy is that Falkenhayn's forces began their attack by employing chlorine gas. The British responded in kind at Loos. Although not proving decisive, gas remained one of the available weapons throughout the remainder of the war.

The inability of the French and the British to achieve success on the Western Front late in 1914 and early in 1915 led to a decision to seek victory elsewhere. They decided upon Gallipoli, a peninsula jutting down from Istanbul adjacent to the Dardanelles, the body of water that links the Black Sea with the Mediterranean and separates the continents of Europe and Asia. Success at Gallipoli would relieve pressure on the Russians and might well compel the Ottoman Empire to withdraw from the war. Success also would boost the morale of the folks back home who, by now, had noticed that, despite huge loss of life, victory was nowhere in sight.

At first, British and French warships attempted to force their way through to Istanbul. That did not work, so the British landed troops ashore in the largest amphibious operation of the war. Among these troops were Australians and New Zealanders. They were known as the ANZACS (the Australian and New Zealand Army Corps) and their exploits at Gallipoli would win them great fame. However, they suffered some 10,000 casualties, for them a substantial number, but a small percentage of the 265,000 Allied troops killed or wounded in an expedition that failed. When the British withdrew in December, no one in the British army or government thought the effort had been other than a debacle.

As the British were departing from Gallipoli, Joffre and the new commander of the BEF, Sir Douglas Haig, were planning their campaigns for 1916. The French general believed in offensive maneuvers and in the imperative of removing German soldiers from French soil. Haig believed the only way to win the war was to attack the German army directly and defeat it. Their plans for 1916 envisioned a series of strikes, straight at and through well-entrenched German positions.

However, Erich von Falkenhayn struck first, preempting Joffre's attacks. In late February, following a massive artillery barrage, the German general sent his troops forward. Their objective was Verdun, a town on the Meuse River some 150 miles northeast of Paris. So began the longest single battle of the First World War. When it was over, 162,440 French soldiers were dead. The number of Germans killed was slightly less.

Falkenhayn had hoped to wear down the French army as to render it ineffective. He came close. But the French commander in charge, Philippe Petain, one the few French generals committed to defensive warfare, led his soldiers confidently and courageously and held Verdun. He earned, as Joffre had at the Marne, the reputation of saving France. Given the battle's outcome, Falkenhayn was relieved of command. His failure at Verdun had worn down the German army instead of the French.

If the First World War is seen as a bloodbath of the first rank, as many people do, the Battle of Verdun is one reason. Another is the Somme.

One hundred and fifty miles long, the river Somme flows through Amiens into the English Channel. The battle to which the river gave its name began in July, 1916 and lasted five months. Haig, a general whom history has not treated well, planned meticulously. His attack was to be preceded by the heaviest artillery barrage the British army could muster: one field gun every 20 yards across a 16-mile front. This was intended to destroy the barbed-wire and machine gun emplacements the enemy were known to have deployed, as well as kill any Germans unfortunate enough to be in range. As the British infantry advanced, their supporting artillery was to move forward, providing covering fire. It was to be a creeping barrage.

The plan was sound. Its execution was not. The British artillery failed in its task. There were too few guns, they were too small in caliber, there were too many shells that did not explode, and the Kaiser's soldiers proved remarkably resilient. For Haig's troops, the results were catastrophic. That first day of July in 1916, 19,000 British soldiers were killed. That number needs to be repeated: 19,000 British soldiers died on the first day of the Somme. Total casualties that day numbered 57,470. The battle continued for another 40 days. Losses piled up for

the Germans as well, and for the French whose Sixth Army
was part of Haig's force.

When the battle came to a close—its official end is
deemed November 18, 1916—the butcher's bill was staggering. Great Britain's official history of the war states that the
combined casualties of the British and French forces totaled
623,907.[4] Of this number, 419,654 were British. All for a neg-
ligible gain in territory. German losses are more difficult to
ascertain, but certainly numbered near to those of their enemy.
As John Keegan has written of the British army, the Somme
"was, and would remain their greatest military tragedy of the
twentieth century, indeed of their national military history."[5]

Yet, the Somme was a victory for the British. Not due to
territory gained, a mere three miles that in no way altered the
strategic picture, but because having themselves suffered horrendous losses, the German army retreated, withdrawing up
to 40 miles in some places. They then completed a system of
strong defensive positions, which the British dubbed the Hindenburg Line. Once there, the Kaiser's army, now with
Hindenburg and Ludendorff in charge, planned no major
offensive. The Somme, wrote an officer on the German General Staff, had been "the muddy grave of the German field
army."[6]

While the German commanders were content to remain
on the defensive, their counterparts in the French and British
armies were not. For them and their troops 1917 would be a
difficult year.

The heavy losses at Verdun had spelled the end of Joffre's
tenure as commander-in-chief of the French army. He was replaced by General Robert Nivelle. An expert in artillery,
Nivelle had performed well at Verdun. In 1917, he persuaded
the French government that he had battlefield tactics that
would bring success against the Germans. He did not. In fact,
his tactics were more of the same: massive artillery strikes across

a narrow front followed by infantry and continuous, rolling cannon fire. Nivelle's offensive began on April 16, 1917. It lasted just five days. The French army got nowhere, but incurred 130,000 casualties. Nivelle and his offensive were disasters. The result was a broken army. More than a few units refused to do further battle. These were the famous mutinies that inflicted the French army in the middle of 1917. Petain was ordered to replace Nivelle and, by improving the lot of the ordinary *poilu*, and by not, for a while, engaging in offensive actions, he was able to restore both discipline and morale. He also had 629 French soldiers condemned to death, but executed only 43.

The British army, too, went on the offensive in 1917, several times. Haig wanted his troops to attack, and attack they did. The first assault occurred at Arras and began on April 9. At first, the British did well, taking 9,000 prisoners and suffering few losses. But, as happened so often in the First World War, the attack stalled, the Germans struck back, and a slugging match became a stalemate. In the end, Haig listed 150,00 men as casualties.

Taking part in the Battle of Arras were four Canadian divisions, some 80,000 men, operating for the first time as the Canadian Corps. Their attack upon Vimy Ridge secured initial success for the British and well deserved fame for Canada and its soldiers. Canadians earned the reputation as tough, no nonsense men of war. For its success at Vimy Ridge, the Canadian Corps' commander, Major General Arthur Currie, was knighted on the battlefield by King George V.

The second British offensive of 1917 took place at Ypres. Its objective was to secure the coast of Belgium thereby denying submarine bases to the German navy. The attack began with 2,229 pieces of artillery opening fire, ten times the number employed at the Somme. The infantry went "over the top" at 3:50 A.M. on July 31. Like Nivelle's offensive, the outcome was disastrous. After four months, 70,000 British soldiers were dead. What made the attack fail was the pervasive rain and mud and, of course, German resistance. Keegan calls the battle "the most notorious land campaign of the war."[7] The battle often goes by the name Passchendaele, a small village outside of Ypres that marked the furthest advance of Haig's army.

The British commander believed the Germans were suffering as much as his army and could less afford the losses. So, Sir Douglas attacked again. This, the third British offensive of 1917, took place at Cambrai, a city northeast of Paris not too far from the border with Belgium. The results followed a familiar pattern: initial success but little gain once the Germans counterattacked. What makes Cambrai significant in military terms is that, for the first time, massed formations of tanks were used. Though slow and prone to mechanical failure, these machines at Cambrai ushered in a new era of land warfare.

FIVE

During 1917, Hindenburg and Ludendorff, Nivelle and Petain, and Douglas Haig commanded troops that engaged in battle, in titanic struggles that help define the First World War. Yet, 1917 also witnessed two events that marked the beginning of the end of the great conflict. One such event took place in Washington, D.C., in April. The other occurred in Berlin.

On January 9, 1917, Germany announced its intention to renew unrestricted submarine warfare. "Unrestricted" meant that no longer would a German *unterseeboot*, or U-boat, refrain from sinking neutral vessels nor allow time for crew to disembark from a ship about to be torpedoed. Beginning in February, any ship would be sunk on sight. Many people were shocked by this announcement. What the Germans were about to do was uncivilized, unnecessarily cruel. But the commanders in Berlin understood that war requires harsh behavior and, besides, submarines had little room for displaced sailors. Moreover, the Kaiser's admirals, and his generals as well, understood that after several years of conflict, such U-boat strikes offered the best chance of winning the war. The goal was to force Britain to withdraw from the war by depriving the island nation of food and essential materials. If Britain were to opt out, France, alone, could be defeated. This goal had to be achieved before the United States entered the war, which it was likely to do once the U-boats began their campaign.

When America joined forces with France and Britain, the battlefield equation would be altered and Germany would lose the war.

Of course, the war at sea had begun well before 1917.

When the German East Asiatic Squadron had to abandon Tsingtao late in 1914, most of its ships sailed across the Pacific Ocean to the coast of Chile. There, under the command of Maximilian von Spee, it destroyed two Royal Navy cruisers, killing 1,600 British sailors. In London, the Admiralty promptly dispatched two battlecruisers, the *Invincible* and the *Inflexible* to deal with von Spee. This they did, totally destroying von Spee's squadron in December.

In 1914, Britain may have had a small army, but it owned a large navy, one which, if it did not rule the waves, came very close to doing so. Upon the declaration of war, the Royal Navy instituted a blockade of Germany. Writing in 1930, Captain B. H. Liddell Hart, a noted military historian, said the blockade "was to do more than any other factor towards winning the war for the Allies."[8] The navy's blockade effectively cut off seaborne traffic to and from German ports. In time, the blockade imposed severe hardship upon the country's industry and civilian population. By 1917, food shortages were causing great distress. As an example, consumption of fish and eggs, once considerable, was reduced by half. By mid-1918, the situation in German cities was such that social unrest was unraveling the political fabric of the Imperial German state.

With its many warships, Britain hoped to lure the Kaiser's quite capable surface fleet into battle. This, it was expected, would result in a great victory, as Trafalgar had been in 1805. In command of the Royal Navy's powerful fleet was Admiral Sir John Jellicoe. On May 31, 1916, he had his chance. The two fleets slugged it out in the North Sea, some 50 miles off the Jutland Peninsula. The statistical results favored the Germans. They lost eleven ships and 3,058 sailors. Jellicoe (whom

Winston Churchill described as the only man in England able to lose the war in an afternoon) had 14 ships sunk and twice that number of men killed. But the battle did not alter the strategic picture. Afterwards the Royal Navy still controlled the seas. Germany's fleet returned to port. Never again did it challenge Britain's maritime preeminence.

Only U-boats could, and would, do that.

German submarines registered their first kill early in the war. On October 20, 1914, U-17 sunk the *Glitra*, a small British ship sailing near Norway.[9] Thereafter, the tempo of attacks quickened. The shipping lanes around the British Isles became dangerous places. On May 7, 1915, in waters close to Ireland, a German submarine put a single torpedo into the starboard side of the Cunard liner *Lusitania,* which then took but 18 minutes to sink. The ship was carrying artillery ammunition for the British army and thus was a legitimate target for U-20. Of the 1,195 fatalities, 123 were American. People in the United States, already angry with Germany over "the Rape of Belgium," were outraged. When months later, more U.S. citizens were killed in a submarine attack, President Woodrow Wilson sent an ultimatum to Berlin: halt unrestricted submarine warfare or the United States would sever diplomatic relations with Germany and, in essence, enter the war on the side of France and Britain. Surprisingly, the Germans did so. But, by 1917, the situation was such that the German High Command reinstated the policy. That year the Kaiser's navy had 111 U-boats in service. Their commanders, armed with skill and courage, as well as torpedoes, intended to destroy the maritime lifeline upon which Great Britain depended. As the number of ships sunk increased, it looked like they would succeed.

Senior officials in London became alarmed. Among them was Jellicoe, who in June 1917 declared that Britain had lost control of the seas. By then First Sea Lord, the top position in the Royal Navy, Jellicoe told his colleagues that Britain would not be able to continue to fight in 1918. Needless to say, this message sent shock waves through the British government. Such pessimism could not be tolerated. Jellico was sacked. More importantly, the navy changed its method of combating submarines.

At first, merchant ships sailed singly. Proposals to group them in an assembly of vessels, a convoy escorted by naval vessels, were rejected. The rationale was that a group of ships would be easier for a U-boat to spot and would overload the capacity of British ports upon reaching its destination. However, both analysis and experience eventually showed that rationale to be flawed. Ports could handle the influx of ships. Moreover, the ocean is so large that a submarine is no more likely to find 40 ships as it would one. And, because the convoy would have Royal Navy ships on guard, success by the U-boats would be limited.

Belatedly, Britain's navy required merchant ships to sail in convoy. This produced the intended result. More and more ships arrived safely. April 1918 was the turning point. From then on, Britain received the supplies needed to continue the war effort.

There was a second failure on the part of the Kaiser's submarines, one that receives less attention than it deserves. They failed to prevent the transport of American soldiers to France. Over two million "doughboys" crossed the Atlantic to serve in the American Expeditionary Force (AEF). All went by ship. Not one of their vessels was sunk. However, what the German submarine campaign did accomplish was America's entry into the war. On April 6, 1917, in Washington, D.C., the United States declared war on Germany.

The United States entered the conflict to save democracy. Added Woodrow Wilson in requesting the declaration:

*We desire no conquest, no dominion. We seek no indem-
nities for ourselves, no material compensation for the sacrifices
we shall freely make. We are but one of the champions of
mankind.* [10]

For Wilson, the enemy was German militarism. America
was to join Britain and France, themselves democratic states,
and rid the world of a government that held in contempt both
freedom and justice. Allied propaganda helped sway the Americans and their president. It portrayed the Germans as
barbarians, a description seemingly verified by their behavior
in Belgium and by their approach to submarine warfare.

Americans were outraged by the sinking of ships without
warning, particularly ships carrying U.S. citizens. They also
were outraged by Germany's foolish effort to tempt Mexico
into the war. Alfred Zimmermann was the Kaiser's foreign
minister. Early in January, 1917 he sent a coded message to the
German ambassador in Mexico suggesting that, in the event of
war between the United States and Germany, Mexico should
side with the latter. Upon the war's conclusion, (with Germany
victorious) Mexico would be rewarded with Texas and other
lands it had once possessed. The British intelligence service
intercepted the message and passed it on to the U.S. Depart-
ment of State. Neither President Wilson nor the American
people took kindly to Zimmermann's intrigue. The result simply was another reason to go to war.

Wilson, who in 1916 had campaigned for reelection by
proclaiming that he had kept America out of the war, had one
additional reason for having the United States enter the
conflict. As Hew Strachan has pointed out, President Wilson
understood that if America were to participate in designing
the postwar world, it would have to do some of the fighting, [11]
and Woodrow Wilson wanted very much to craft that future
world. Indeed, he had at least 14 ideas as to how to do it.

Six

Both then and now, the army the United States deployed to France in 1917 and 1918 was called the American Expeditionary Force (AEF). Its commander was General John J. Pershing.

Known as "Black Jack" because he once had commanded African-American soldiers, Pershing was a combat veteran of the war with Spain and of the insurrection in the Philippines. In 1916, he led an expedition into Mexico in search of Pancho Villa, who had raided several towns in the United States. Pershing was a tough, demanding officer respected by his men, but not beloved. His career, no doubt, had been helped by having a father-in-law who was chairman of the Senate's Military Affairs Committee.

Arriving in France in June, 1917 (it was an aide to Pershing not the general who said, "Lafayette, we are here") Pershing had to assemble, supply, and train a force capable of taking on the Kaiser's battle-tested army. This was no easy task, for the Americans getting off the ships were neither well prepared nor properly equipped. The AEF had no artillery, no tanks, no airplanes and no machine guns. The men themselves were little more than raw recruits. Many had never fired their weapons. To turn them into a combat ready army required time and instruction. It also required equipment, much of which was purchased from the French. Pershing was able to buy what he needed. The AEF bought 3,532 artillery pieces; 40,884 automatic weapons; 227 tanks; and 4,874 aircraft from French suppliers.[12] When the Americans finally went into battle, they did so because French manufacturers had provided much of their equipment.

Training was also provided by the French, as well as by the British. Veterans of combat, these instructors taught the Americans how to survive and fight in the hellish world of trenches, barbed-wire, mud, poison gas, machine guns, and deadly artillery fire.

Pershing himself wanted the Americans to emphasize the rifle and the bayonet. His war fighting doctrine stressed marksmanship and maneuver. He envisioned the AEF making quick frontal assaults then breaking through German defenses and advancing rapidly, destroying the enemy as it moved forward. That this approach made little sense in the environment of the Western Front appeared not to register with General Pershing. It certainly made an impact on the average American soldier. Many of them died or were wounded needlessly. The consensus seems to be that the number of casualties suffered by the AEF, 255,970, was larger than it should have been.

By war's end, the American Expeditionary Force had grown to just over two million men. In total, including those stationed stateside, the United States Army numbered 3,680,458. This was a staggering increase over the 208,034 that constituted the army in early 1917, at which point the American army ranked sixteenth in size, just behind Portugal.

Transporting the AEF to France was no easy task. It was done by ship, of course, and took time. More than one senior official in London and Paris wondered whether the Americans were ever to arrive. True, at first the buildup was slow, but by the summer of 1918, 14 months after Congress declared war, U.S. troops were pouring into France.

French and British generals wanted the arriving soldiers

to be allocated to their armies. The Yanks were to replenish Allied regiments depleted by three years of warfare. The generals reasoned that the Americans not only lacked combat experience, they also lacked staff organization essential to large military units. Developing these staffs, gaining the necessary experience would take time, valuable time. Better, they argued, to place the Americans among experienced French and British troops, and do so right away. Waiting for a fully prepared, independent American army risked defeat on the battlefield. Time was of the essence. The best way to utilize American soldiers was to distribute them among seasoned troops already on the front line.

Pershing said no. Though directed by the Secretary of War to cooperate with the French and the British, the commander of the AEF was ordered to field an independent American army and to lead it into battle. This is exactly what he did.

Senior French and British generals, several of whom thought Pershing was not up to his job, frequently tried to have the American troops amalgamated into their armies. And, just as frequently, Black Jack replied that Americans had come to France to fight as an American army, pointing out, probably correctly, that U.S. soldiers likely were to fight best under American officers in an army whose flag was the Stars and Stripes.

Yet, again to Pershing's credit, when in May–June 1918 a battlefield crisis arose, and both General Ferdinand Foch and Field Marshal Sir Douglas Haig urgently needed additional troops, Pershing dispatched several U.S. divisions to bolster French and British forces.

The principal fighting unit of the AEF was the division. At 28,000 men, it was twice the size of British and French counterparts. All 43 divisions that served in France were infantry divisions. While an AEF division would have its own artillery and support units, plus 6,638 horses and mules, its principal component was the rifleman.[13] The United States entered the war deficient in modern weaponry. As previously noted, the AEF lacked artillery, aircraft, tanks, and machine guns. What it did possess, and what it did contribute, was manpower. By the summer of 1918, the French army was worn out. The British army, still ready for battle, was running out of men. Pershing's army represented a vast influx of men, men whose number and willingness to fight would play a decisive role in the outcome of the First World War.

Two of the 43 divisions of the AEF were composed of Black Americans. These were newly raised units, the 93rd and 92nd divisions. The former was lent to the French army and fought extremely well. One of the 93rd's regiments, the 369th "Black Rattlers" served with great distinction, particularly in the September, 1918 attack upon the town of Sechault receiving for its efforts the French medal of valor, the Croix de Guerre. The 92nd had less success. It remained in the AEF and went into battle in September as well. Due mostly to poor leadership and incomplete training, the division performed poorly. This, unfortunately, left a legacy in the American army. Throughout the postwar years, the army's officer corps were skeptical of the ability of African-Americans to both command and fight.

Racism was a fact of life in America during the years of the First World War. This permeated the nation's army wherein Blacks usually were given jobs of secondary importance. In 1916, there were four "colored" regiments in the regular army. None of them served in France. However, some 200,000 other African-American soldiers were part of the American Expeditionary Force. Yet most of these men were put to work in what essentially were labor battalions, digging ditches and unloading ships. This, despite the fact that U.S. authorities had established an officer training school for Blacks in Des Moines, Iowa that produced 1,100 officers for the United States Army.

Women, too, faced discrimination in the army. Given that in 1917-1918 they did not have the right to vote, this is not surprising. About 10,000 women served as nurses in the AEF. Though treated as officers, they were not paid as such. Nor, according to historian Byron Farwell, did the army provide them with uniforms or equipment.[14] Those came from the Red Cross. Despite the inequity, the women's services were indispensable and performed with skill and dedication.

Also performing essential medical services were Americans who, prior to the United States' entry into the war, drove ambulances for the French military. They were volunteers, many of them students or graduates of America's finest colleges. Serving as non-combatants, they transported wounded French soldiers from the battlefield to the hospital. Over 2,000 young men so volunteered, eventually carrying some 400,000 soldiers to safety.

Nurses were not the only group of women attached to the AEF. To operate the telephone switchboard established at corps and army headquarters, Pershing recruited over 200 women fluent in French. Trained by the American Telephone and Telegraph Company in Illinois, they were attached to the army's Signal Corps. After purchasing their uniforms in New York, they were shipped to France and went to work. Known as the "Hello Girls," they provided yeoman service and received praise from Pershing himself. What they did not receive were official discharge papers, medals, or veteran benefits. They were bluntly informed that, despite their uniforms and services, they were employees of the army, not members. Thus, they were not entitled to benefits given to the men of the AEF. Not until 1979 was this injustice rectified, by which time, of course, it was too late for most of these women.

If America's army required months and months to prepare for battle, its navy did not. On May 4, 1917, just 28 days after the United States declared war, six American destroyers dropped anchor in Queenstown Harbor on the southern coast of Ireland. They and the others that followed would provide needed protection to the merchant ships sailing to and from Britain. Heavier naval firepower arrived in December. Five battleships of the United States Navy, all commanded by Rear Admiral Hugh Rodman, joined the Royal Navy's Grand Fleet. Significantly, they served under British command and were present when Germany's High Seas Fleet surrendered.

The United States Navy's role in the First World War is overshadowed by that of Pershing's army. For most Americans, the image of the conflict is that of soldiers in trenches surrounded by mud and barbed-wire. The navy's contribution receives little notice. Even less attention is given to Admiral William S. Sims who throughout the war was in charge of American naval operations in Europe.

In addition to dispatching destroyers and battleships to England, America's navy established a special task force consisting primarily of cruisers that escorted the ships transporting the AEF to France. The navy also provided its air service to the war effort. This comprised some 500 aircraft distributed among 26 naval air stations located in Britain, France, and Italy. And, rather remarkably, it sent five very heavy, large naval guns mounted on railroad cars to France where, in the Allied offensives of September 1918, they pounded German positions near Soissons.

One other achievement of America's navy in World War One deserves mention. As part of the effort to stymie German submarines, the Royal Navy proposed to lay a barrier of mines from northern Scotland across the North Sea to southern Norway. This would seal off the northern perimeter of the North Sea (a similar barrier was to be laid down across the

English Channel near Dover). The project would deny the U-boats free access to the Atlantic Ocean. This was to be an enormous undertaking. Two factors initially delayed its start: the Royal Navy had few ships to spare, and, perhaps more importantly, British mines were defective. Enter the United States Navy. In June 1918, it began laying its own mines. In total, the Americans put 56,571 mines into the water. Britain's navy laid 13,546.[15] Together they were strung along an underwater belt some 200 miles long. Jellicoe's successor, Admiral David Beatty, opposed the project. He said it would hinder operations of the fleet and consume resources better spent elsewhere. He had a point. The barrier, the Northern Barrage, to use its customary name, accounted for the destruction of but six U-boats.

Most German submarines operated in the waters around Great Britain and in the Mediterranean. Few made war patrols to North America. One that did was U-156. On July 19, 1918, off the coast of Long Island, the cruiser *USS San Diego* sank, having struck a mine laid by the German submarine. The cruiser was the only major American warship lost in World War One.

SEVEN

In returning to unrestricted submarine warfare in 1917, Germany had gambled that it could force Great Britain out of the war before America's involvement made much of a difference. The gamble failed. In 1914, Germany gambled that it could destroy the French army in 40 days before having to move east against the Tsar. This gamble also failed. Four years later, in 1918, Germany would take one last gamble.

Hindenburg and Ludendorff, by now running the government as well as the army, decided upon one final offensive in the west. It would be a massive affair, employing especially trained storm-troopers and army units no longer needed on the Russian Front. The attack began on March 21, starting with a thunderous barrage of artillery delivered by 6,473 guns. Three separate German armies struck hard crushing the British Fifth Army, one of four units under Sir Douglas Haig's command. That first day the Kaiser's men killed 7,000 British soldiers and took 21,000 prisoners. The attack was a stunning success. The Germans advanced 40 miles, a significant distance, before the British were able to stop them.

A second offensive took place in Flanders, the Germans attacking early in April. Here, too, they made progress forcing the British commander-in-chief to issue his famous "backs to the walls" directive. Sir Douglas instructed his soldiers not to retreat, to hold on whatever the cost. His order was taken to heart. Here are parts of the written orders a young Australian officer issued to his men:

1. *This position will be held and the section will remain here until relieved.*
2. *The enemy cannot be allowed to interfere with this program.*
3. *If the section cannot remain here alive it will remain here dead, but in any case it will remain here.*
4. *If any man through shell shock or other cause attempts to surrender he will remain here dead.*[16]

The men given this order obeyed. The order was found on the body of one of their dead.

In their spring offensives, the Germans also struck the French. Ludendorff, who planned the attacks, sent his troops to the Chemin des Dames sector, to the northeast of Reims. They crushed the French Sixth Army and advanced to the Marne River, again threatening Paris. In June and July, the Germans, for the fourth and fifth time, attacked once more. These were less successful. Nonetheless, French forces had been battered. French troops were in retreat.

All along the Front, German troops moved forward, inflicting an enormous number of casualties. In just the first 40 days of combat, Sir Douglas Haig's forces suffered over 160,000 killed or wounded. French losses in the spring and summer reached 70,000. The British and French armies were bleeding, and bleeding badly.

As the casualties mounted and the German advances continued, top Allied leaders realized that a change in the military command structure was needed. Heretofore, the senior French and British field commanders, at the time Petain and Haig, and earlier, Nivelle and Haig, acted independently. They consulted with one another, but neither could command the other. The German spring offensives changed that. All came to understand that a single field commander-in-chief needed to be in charge. Such was the urgency that Field Marshal Haig raised no objection to the appointment of French general Ferdinand Foch to the post (Petain was considered too defensively oriented). The French general became, as Eisenhower would in the Second World War, Supreme Allied Commander. At first, he was only to coordinate the three armies involved, the British, French and American. But, as the German threat increased, Foch was authorized to give orders to their commanders. Only if Haig and Pershing considered these orders detrimental to the national interests of Great Britain or the United States were the two subordinate commanders allowed to appeal. Petain had no such authority; he was told to follow Foch's instructions. Despite disagreements, some rather testy, this new command arrangement proved satisfactory. Ferdinand Foch, the general who believed the only military course of action worthy of consideration was to attack, became commander of over five million men. Given his preeminent position in the chain of command and his subsequent record of success it's not surprising that upon his death in 1920, his body was laid to rest in Paris near that of Napoleon.

As spring gave way to summer, the German offensives appeared to stall. Though inflicting heavy losses upon their French and British counterparts, the Germans themselves suffered as well. By the end of April, in just two months, 492,720 of their soldiers no longer were able to fight. They were dead, in a hospital, missing in action, or taken prisoner. More German soldiers would be lost in May and June, and into July when, finally, after the fourth and fifth attacks, the offensive came to a halt. In total, Ludendorff's spring offensives cost the Kaiser 800,000 of his soldiers.

Moreover, the British army, though roughed up, had not been destroyed. Sir Douglas' men, by 1918 the most capable fighting force in Europe, had bent but not broken. So too, the French. Petain's army, one that had experienced both victory and defeat in four years of conflict, still had some fight left in it.

As, of course, did the Germany army. Yet, it was clear, especially to Foch, that the German spring offensives had failed. True, Ludendorff's men had gained considerable territory, but no decisive victory had been won, nor had the strategic picture changed much. The Front, that tangled strip of trenches, barbed-wire and machine gun nests, had been moved to the west. Save for some worried souls in Paris, nothing much seemed to have changed.

In fact, two things had changed, both significant. The first was that the German army was running out of soldiers. A country can produce only a certain number of men capable of bearing arms and, by the summer of 1918, after fighting Russians and Romanians, the British and the French, Germany had just about reached its limit. And later, replacement troops were not as skillful as those who had fought earlier in the war. The second change to the situation, one even more ominous to Ludendorff and his field commanders, was that Pershing's American Expeditionary Force was preparing to do battle.

EIGHT

The AEF's first test of combat had come in late May, 1918. Assigned to French forces, the U.S. Army's 1st Division was given the task of taking Cantigny. This was a small village on a ridge near Montdidier, a town some 60 miles north of Paris. The ridge enabled the Germans to observe what was taking place to the south and west of their positions. Planning the attack was the division's operations officer, Lt. Colonel George C. Marshall. Well conceived and twice rehearsed, the plan had the division's 28th Infantry Regiment directly assaulting the town supported by artillery, tanks, and flamethrowers all provided by the French.

The attack began early in the morning of May 28, 1918. By noon, the village was in U.S. hands. The Germans counterattacked, several times, and the battle became what author David Bonk has called "a desperate slugging match."[17] Showing notable determination, the men of the 28th held on, despite the premature withdrawal of the French artillery. When the battle was over, the regiment sustained more than 900 casualties. More importantly, Cantigny remained under U.S. control.

The town itself was of no overall strategic value to the Allies. But the fight for Cantigny was important. It demonstrated that the AEF could plan and execute a division-level operation. It also showed that despite their inexperience, individual American soldiers would do just fine in battle. French

and Britain commanders were uncertain how Pershing's soldiers would respond to the ordeal of battle. So, too, were
German commanders who tried to convince their troops and
themselves that Americans were no match for well-disciplined
and battle-tested German soldiers. The fight for Cantigny put
to rest such nonsense. For Foch and Haig it was reassuring. For
Ludendorff it was cause for concern. For General Pershing and
his troops, and for the folks back home in the USA, it was a
signal that once fully deployed, the American Expeditionary
Force would have soldiers to be reckoned with.

As the 1st Division's fight at Cantigny came to a close, the
AEF's 3rd Division was moving into action. Ludendorff's May
offensive, code-named Blucher, had seen much success with
the Germans reaching the Marne. The French, dispirited by
their enemy's advances, asked General Pershing for assistance.
Recognizing the urgency of the situation, Black Jack put aside
his objection to amalgamation and lent the 3rd Division to the
French. They ordered it to Chateau Thierry. This was (and still
is) a lovely little town on the Marne River, today the site of an
American military cemetery. At Chateau Thierry the Americans held fast and Ludendorff's troops advanced no further.

Not far from Chateau Thierry, to the west, were two
villages, Bouresches and Belleau. In between them stood a
small forest. It was called Belleau Wood. In June 1918 it witnessed a fierce battle, one that for the United States of America
would become legendary.

That same month, still needing to slow the German advance, Foch requested additional American help. However, he
planned not just to halt the German drive. Foch planned to
counterattack and wanted some of Pershing's troops to participate. The AEF responded by lending Foch the 2nd Division,
which the French deployed to Belleau Wood. This unit was
unique in the American Expeditionary Force in that two of its

four infantry regiments, comprising the 4th Brigade, were United States marines, not soldiers of the U.S. Army.

The 4th Brigade's first task was to stop a German attack, which it did. The story is told that a retreating French officer said to an American that with the Germans advancing, he and his men should fall back. "Retreat, hell," replied the marine, "we just got here."

The second task assigned to the marines was to clear Belleau Wood of Germans and hold onto it. On June 6 they attacked. Their artillery was insufficient, their tactics flawed. But, as the marines crossed a wheat field full of red poppies, their determination and courage were in full view. The attack succeeded although the cost was high. The brigade's casualties that day totaled 1,087. The fight would continue for 20 more days and, at times, the marines took no prisoners, nor did the Germans. It was kill or be killed.

Towards the end of the struggle for Belleau Wood, the 2nd Division's other brigade, the one consisting of two army regiments, went into action. It was ordered to capture the nearby town of Vaux. Quite competently the brigade took control of the town, for its effort suffering 300 dead and 1,400 wounded. This battle at Vaux received little attention. In 1918, and even today, what captured the spotlight were the marines at Belleau Wood.

By the standards of the First World War, the engagements of Belleau Wood and Vaux were small affairs. In total, the casualty count for the U.S. 2nd Division showed 1,811 men dead and 7,966 wounded. For the armies of France, Great Britain, and Germany these were numbers unlikely to raise alarm. For the AEF, 9,777 in one division was a stiff price. It illustrated that inexperience on the battlefield costs lives. Nonetheless, Vaux and Belleau Wood were victories. As did Cantigny, the two battles bode well for the Allied cause.

The next occasion in which the AEF went into action in-

volved far more men than had fought at Vaux and Belleau
Wood. Once the German spring offensive came to a halt, Ferdinand Foch was keen to strike back. He wanted to recover
territory lost to the Germans and he also wanted to damage
Ludendorff's army, which he believed by then to be under
considerable stress. He directed Petain to prepare a plan of
attack, which the French army's commander-in-chief did. The
plan included substantial participation by the Americans.

Two U.S. divisions, along with a French Moroccan unit,
spearheaded the attack. They were part of the French Tenth
Army. Pershing had once again agreed to allocate American
units to Petain's forces. Three other AEF divisions were
assigned to the French Sixth Army while a further three were
part of the force held in reserve. Ultimately, some 300,000
American soldiers were involved. The attack, along a 25-mile
front in the vicinity of Soissons, began on July 18. It was over
by August 2. Approximately 30,000 Germans were taken prisoner. Such was the success that, afterward, the Kaiser's son
wrote his father that the war was lost.

This battle is usually referred to as the Second Battle of
the Marne, a name that includes the earlier unsuccessful effort
to halt the German advance that had brought the Kaiser's army
to the river's edge. One key result of this battle was Ludendorff's decision to call off a major attack against the British in
the north. The German commander had hoped, once and for
all, to crush Field Marshal Haig's forces in France. That had
been the decisive victory Ludendorff had designed his spring
offensives to achieve.

Meanwhile, Sir Douglas had planned an offensive of his
own, one to which Foch as Supreme Commander readily
agreed. On August 8, the British army attacked near Amiens.
Among the assault troops were Canadians and Australians,
whom the West Point Military History Series account of
World War One says were, "generally regarded as the finest

infantry fighters on the Allied side."[18] The outcome was a stunning success for British arms. Haig's losses were light, suggesting that the British at last had mastered the art of trench warfare. German losses were substantial. Some 70,000 troops were put out of action. Of these, 30,000 had surrendered without much of a fight. In his memoir, Ludendorff, who offered to resign after the battle, termed August 8 "the black day of the German army."[19]

The British victory at Amiens was one of the more decisive battles of the First World War, but not because of territory gained or men lost. Rather, it was important because of its psychological impact upon the Germans. After Amiens, the German high command realized that defeat was now likely. For Germany the war was lost once its generals believed the war was lost. After their drubbing by the British in August 1918, that's exactly what they began to believe.

Two days after the British launched their attack from Amiens, the American Expeditionary Force established a new combat organization. Previously, the AEF had been organized into divisions as its primary fighting units. As we've seen, these went into battle as components of various French armies. By August, however the number of American divisions had increased so as to warrant a larger combat unit. On August 10, 1918, the First United States Army was brought into being. It consisted of 14 divisions organized into three corps. Its commander was John J. Pershing, who remained in charge of the AEF, of which First Army became the principal American combat unit.

By early October, the number of American soldiers justified the establishment of the U.S. Second Army. Its commander was Major General Robert Lee Bullard, who had been in charge of the 1st Division at Cantigny. By then, First Army had a new commander. He was Hunter Liggett, also a major general. Both Liggett and Bullard reported to Pershing,

who then was at the same level as Field Marshal Sir Douglas
Haig and General Phillippe Petain, each of whose commands
encompassed several separate armies. Above Haig, Petain, and
Pershing was the Supreme Commander, Ferdinand Foch.

In early September, Foch had been content to have Allied
troops conduct limited offensives along the entire Western
Front. For the AEF this involved the elimination of the St. Mihiel salient. In military terminology, a salient is a wedge, a
protrusion in the battle line often shaped like an arrowhead. In
1914, the Germans had created such a wedge 16 miles deep
into the French lines with the tip of the salient at a small town
well to the east of Paris. Several times the French army had
attempted to eliminate it. Each time the army had failed.

The St. Mihiel salient was in the American sector of operations. Not surprisingly, General Pershing decided to have
his First American Army remove the wedge. Initially, he
planned to have the army continue on to Metz, then a heavily
fortified German stronghold. Such a move, if successful, would
have had strategic consequences, by threatening the position of
all German forces on the Western Front. Foch, however, inter-
vened. He wanted Pershing to abandon the attack upon St.
Mihiel and strike northwest into the Meuse-Argonne rather
than northeast towards Metz. The Supreme Commander also
wanted to insert a French army in the attack and place some
of the American troops under French command. Pershing re-
acted strongly to both proposals and the conversation between
the two commanders became heated. The result was a com-
promise. The American army would move against the salient,
but not proceed beyond it. And, it would do so with fewer
troops. But, acceding to Foch's desires, the United States First
Army, with a large number of soldiers, then would advance
into the Meuse-Argonne, striking northwest as the Supreme
Commander wished.

The attack upon the salient began on September 12 with

an artillery barrage from 3,010 guns. Then, seven U.S. infantry divisions struck from the east. One American division attacked from the west while French units advanced at the tip. In total, 500,000 American soldiers went into battle with 100,000 French troops. Within two days the salient was reduced. Pershing's men took 13,000 prisoners and captured a large number of enemy guns. American casualties numbered approximately 7,000.

Among the artillery pieces employed were the 14-inch naval guns. Mounted on railroad cars, they shot a projectile up to 23 miles and, if on target, were devastating to the enemy. The challenge, of course, was in correctly aiming the gun and properly gaging the ballistics of the projectile. At first, the gunners had difficulty in hitting some of their targets. Help came from a young army captain, Edwin P. Hubble, who understood mathematics and the science of trajectories.[20] He later became an astronomer of note, winning a Nobel Prize. When in 1990 the American space agency, NASA, placed a powerful telescope in low earth orbit, the instrument was named for Dr. Hubble.

St. Mihiel was an American victory and was celebrated as such. Once again, as at Cantigny, Chateau Thierry, and Belleau Wood, the AEF troops had fought hard. Indeed, the German high command took note of the Americans' aggressive spirit. But the sense of victory from St. Mihiel must be tempered. It is generally conceded that a more experienced army would have taken a greater number of prisoners. Additionally, the German army, aware of the forthcoming assault and of its vulnerability within the salient, had begun to withdraw. The fight was not as fierce as it might have been. Nonetheless, the American First Army had gone into battle and won.

Next time, at the Meuse-Argonne, the fight would be far more difficult.

NINE

Noteworthy in the attack upon the salient at St. Mihiel was the widespread use of aircraft. Over 1,400 airplanes took part in the operation. They were flown by American, British, and French pilots (and a few Italians). In command of this aerial armada was Colonel Billy Mitchell who, postwar, would become a leading advocate of American air power.

The airplane came of age in the First World War. Armies and navies too, saw opportunities in the use of aircraft. They pushed aeronautical technologies such that planes became faster, more versatile, and somewhat more reliable. They also became weapons of war. Machine guns were carried, though at first their impact was slight. But, when interrupter gears were developed so that machine guns could be fired safely through spinning propellers, airplanes became efficient killing machines.

These machines were called pursuit planes, what today are termed fighters. They carried a crew of one, the pilot, and could attain speeds of up to 140 mph. In Germany and Britain, in America and France, and in other countries as well, pursuit pilots became national heroes, especially those who destroyed five enemy aircraft, thus winning the coveted (but unofficial) title of ace. Famous still today is the German ace Manfred von Richtofen, the Red Baron. His score of 80 kills was the highest tally of any pilot in World War One. The leading American ace was Eddie Rickenbacker who, flying French-built aircraft, knocked down 26 German planes.

Despite the fame associated with pursuit pilots, they and their aircraft did not play a decisive role in the war. Nor did the bombers. These were larger machines, multi-engine, with a crew of three or four. From 1915 on, they were heavily engaged, bombing enemy troops and installations. But, the size and number of bombs they could carry were slight and the accuracy of their aim uneven. So they, too, played a secondary role.

However, one particular bomber is worth mentioning. This is the German Gotha G IV. Powered by two Mercedes six-cylinder engines, the airplane had a top speed of 88 mph at 12,000 feet. More noteworthy was its range. The Gotha could fly from Ghent, Belgium to London, England and back, which it did on more than one occasion. As did German Zeppelins, rigid-framed airships. Together, they constituted the first ever effort at strategic bombing. Though they killed some 1,500 people in England, the damage they caused was insignificant. Their principal impact was to alarm civil and military authorities forcing both to devise appropriate defenses and, with good cause, to worry about what the future might bring.

The one function performed by aircraft during World War One that did make a difference on the battlefield was reconnaissance. Airplanes were used to locate enemy positions and to track the movement of enemy troops. In 1914-1918 these planes usually were two-seaters. Up front was the pilot. To his rear was the observer who, when the need arose, also functioned as a gunner. Occasionally, observation aircraft proved decisive. In 1914, for example, they alerted Joffre to the gap between the German First and Second Armies as the two enemy forces approached the Marne.

Later in the war, observers would employ specially developed cameras with which to photograph the enemy. On both sides aerial photography was extensive. Such was the extent of this activity that a principal function of pursuit planes was the destruction of enemy aircraft devoted to observation.

Another important task given to observation aircraft was spotting for artillery. The soldiers who fired the cannons needed to know where their shells were striking. Many times in the course of the war, they were so informed by aircraft aloft for that very purpose.

The first Americans who fought in the sky did so as part of the French Air Service. Many of these initially served as ambulance drivers in units supporting the French army. Indeed, the first Americans to see the ugly face of war transported wounded French soldiers to medical facilities in the rear. They had arrived in France well before the United States entered the war in 1917. Such was their service that 225 of them won citations of valor. No recounting of America's involvement in the First World War is complete without mention of their work.

In April 1916, the French Air Service established a squadron of pursuit planes piloted primarily by Americans. Like the ambulance drivers, these pilots were volunteers. Eventually, 38 Americans flew in this squadron, which became known as the Lafayette Escadrille. With French officers in charge, the squadron flew over 3,000 sorties and downed in excess of 50 enemy aircraft. One of the Escadrille pilots, Raoul Lufbery, an American born in France, was an ace with 17 victories to his credit. Once the United States entered the war, the Lafayette Escadrille ceased to exist, becoming the 103rd Aero Squadron of the American Air Service. Three months later Lufbery was gone. He jumped (or fell) to his death from a burning aircraft. Pilots back then did not wear parachutes.

In both France and the United States, the Lafayette Escadrille won great fame, not just for its exploits in combat, nor because its mascots were two cute lion cubs named

Whiskey and Soda. The squadron gained prominence because it represented the desire of many Americans to aid France in that country's hour of need. As time passed and the war continued, more Americans joined the French Air Service, many serving with distinction. Today, David Putnam, Frank Baylies, and Tom Cassady are names no longer remembered. But each flew for France to the regret of more than a few German aviators.

American pilots also flew in British squadrons, even after the AEF arrived in Europe. Forty-one of them scored five kills or more. Among these pilots was Howard Burdick. He flew the Sopwith Camel, considered by many to be the best of the Allied pursuit planes. Burdick downed six enemy aircraft in September and October of 1918. Years later, during the Second World War, his son Clinton destroyed nine German planes while piloting a P-51 Mustang of the American Eighth Air Force.

In both Great Britain and America, in France and Germany, pursuit pilots were considered to be men of dash and daring, knights of the sky who bravely confronted the enemy in airborne chariots. Less attention was given to their victims, of whom there were many. The top eight French aces of World War One, for example, killed at least 339 German flyers. These men joined 7,873 others of the Kaiser's air service who did not survive the war.[21] Britain's Royal Flying Corps and Royal Naval Air Service, combined in 1918 to form the Royal Air Force, counted 9,378 men who died in their aerial operations. Many of these were boys of 19 or 20, whose flying skills were limited. Due to the demand for pilots, they had been rushed into battle. Needless to say, their chances of survival were slim. This unhappy situation is well portrayed in the 1938 classic film *Dawn Patrol*, in which a young rookie British pilot, David Niven's onscreen brother, is sent into battle by the squadron's commander, played by Errol Flynn. Both Niven's and Flynn's characters realize the young pilot is ill-prepared for combat and will not return alive.

The United States had but 237 flyers killed in combat (one of the dead was Quentin Roosevelt, youngest son of Theodore Roosevelt). The number is small, reflecting the limited time the AEF spent at the Front. Nonetheless, America's Army Air Service performed extremely well. Its pursuit pilots accounted for the destruction of 781 enemy aircraft, losing 289 of their own.[22] As the U.S. produced no combat planes of its own, American pilots flew machines designed and built in Britain and France. The latter included both the Nieuport 17 and the SPAD XIII, two aircraft the Americans used to good advantage.

Frank Luke was one of these pilots. He flew the SPAD XIII, a fine machine that by war's end equipped most U.S. Air Service units. SPAD was the acronym for the French company that produced the airplane: *Societe Pour L'Aviation et ses Derives*. Hailing from Arizona, Luke served with the 27th Aero Squadron, destroying 18 enemy machines in September 1918. On the 29th of that month, he was shot down by ground fire. His SPAD crashed in enemy territory. Wounded but still very much alive, Frank Luke drew his pistol and fired at the Germans. They fired back and killed him. Today, Luke Air Force Base in Arizona honors his fighting spirit.

Several of the enemy machines Frank Luke destroyed were observation balloons. Tethered to the ground, these reached heights of up to 5,000 feet. With a crew, usually two men, balloons were employed by both sides to monitor the enemy's whereabouts. Filled with gas, often hydrogen, balloons were frequent targets of pursuit planes. But they were not easy to take down. At their base were numerous anti-aircraft guns just waiting for enemy aircraft to appear. Attacking observation balloons, therefore, was a hazardous venture. Manning them also was dangerous. When struck by incendiary bullets the balloons burst into flames creating a spectacular fireball. Unlike pursuit pilots, however, balloon crews were issued parachutes. The crew's challenge was to jump neither too soon nor too late.

TEN

Observation balloons were in full use when British, French and American armies began the great offensive that at last would bring about the end of the war. Many in leadership positions in both France and Britain thought the war would continue well into 1919. Not Foch. He believed that a massive attack across the entire Western Front in September would crush the German army. After all, he reasoned, the Allies outmatched their enemy in soldiers, supplies, tanks, and aircraft. Accordingly, the Supreme Commander drew up a plan of battle that was complex in detail, yet simple in concept: the British (and Belgians) would strike in the north, the French would advance in the middle, while the Americans would attack in the south, in the area known as the Meuse-Argonne. With characteristic energy, Ferdinand Foch proclaimed, "*Tout le monde a la bataille.*"[23]

The Meuse is a major river, 575 miles long, that flows from northeastern France through Verdun into Belgium and Holland, eventually draining into the North Sea. The Argonne is a region of France, much of it heavily wooded, east of Paris through which the Meuse flows. In 1918, the area was well fortified by the German army.

The assault by Pershing's army began on September 26, with an artillery barrage purposefully kept brief in order to maintain surprise (one of the artillery batteries was captured by a young officer from Missouri by the name of Harry S. Truman). Nineteen divisions took part, six of them French. That meant that Black Jack Pershing commanded over 1.2 million soldiers. The campaign lasted 47 days and was hard fought. One German officer wrote, "The Americans are here. We can kill them but not stop them."[24]

Throughout the battle, the AEF's inexperience showed. At times, supplies ran short and tactics were flawed. Transportation was chaotic. Yet, Pershing drove his men forward, relieving commanders he considered insufficiently aggressive. Many Americans fought tenaciously. Among them were the "Black Ratters" of the 369th Infantry Regiment, the African-American unit previously mentioned. A few did not. When the American attack stalled, Foch proposed to insert additional French troops in the sector and turn overall command to a French general. Pershing refused and simply continued the assault. By early November, his troops had thrown the Germans back. In the process, the AEF had inflicted some 100,000 casualties upon the enemy and taken 26,000 prisoners. American historian Edward G. Lengel said that the French army could not have done what the Americans accomplished.[25]

Lengel also says that the British army could have and would have done so with fewer casualties, for the losses of the American army at the Meuse-Argonne were high. The American dead numbered 26,277. The number of American wounded totaled 95,923. Writes Lengel in his 2008 book on the Meuse-Argonne campaign,

> . . . many doughboys died unnecessarily because of foolishly brave officers who led their men head-on against enemy machine guns.[26]

Casualties aside, the Americans clearly had gained a victory. Pershing's men had battled a German army and won.

Despite this victory, one noted British military historian

calls the Meuse-Argonne campaign unnecessary. In his book on World War One, H. P. Willmott writes that the battle should not have been fought at all.[27] Why? Because to the north, British armies had breached the Hindenburg Line.

As did Foch, Sir Douglas Haig believed the war need not continue into 1919. He thought a strong Allied push in September and October would bring the war to a successful conclusion. By then, Haig commanded five field armies. Together they represented the most capable military force in Europe.

On September 27, the British attacked. The assault began with a huge artillery barrage, with one gun for every three yards of territory to be attacked. Thirty-three divisions took part, two of them American. The British forces smashed into their opponents, delivering a blow from which the Germans could not recover.

For Ludendorff and Hindenburg, September brought additional bad news. As American, French and British troops gained success on the Western Front, an Allied army composed of British, French and Serbian soldiers, all under the command of French general Franchet d'Esperey, advanced from Salonika in Greece into Serbia and Bulgaria. The latter was an important ally of Germany. Bulgaria was a land bridge to the Ottomans and gave Germany a position of strength in the Balkans. The Allied army met with such success that Bulgaria withdrew from the war.

The Ottoman Empire, too, was in trouble. In Palestine, British forces were defeating the Turks while, along the southern Alps, the Italians at long last were gaining ground against the Austrians.

Everywhere Ludendorff and Hindenburg looked, they saw defeat. Inside Germany, the news was equally grim. In cities across the country, shortages of coal, soap, and food caused ordinary Germans to be cold, dirty, and hungry. In Berlin, such shortages and the lack of military success brought about rioting in the streets. In fact, the German Imperial State was disintegrating. Both political moderates and right-wingers feared a Bolshevik-styled revolution. In Kiel and Wilhelmshaven, German admirals ordered the High Seas Fleet to sortie for one last glorious battle, but its sailors mutinied. The navy thus imploded, while the army high command concluded that the war could not be won. On October 1, Ludendorff told the German foreign minister to seek an immediate armistice. Days later, Hindenburg conveyed a note to the new chancellor, Prince Max of Baden, that called the situation acute. Earlier, on September 29, the two generals, the most senior in the army, had told the Kaiser the fighting had to stop.

There followed an attempt by the German government to seek an armistice through the good offices of America's president. Prince Max and others assumed that Germany could secure a better deal were the terms first worked out with the Americans. After all, in January 1918, in a speech to Congress, Wilson—a true idealist—had outlined Fourteen Points that he thought should serve as the basis for constructing the postwar world. However, Wilson's response surprised the Germans. Angered by the harm he believed German militarism had inflicted upon the world, and by Germany's continuation of unrestricted submarine warfare, Wilson held firm. His terms were tough. Among them was the requirement that the Kaiser had to go. Regarding an end to the fighting, President Wilson told the Germans to speak with Foch.

In early November, with the concurrence of the army, Prince Max sent emissaries to the Allied Supreme Commander. They were to discuss terms for an armistice.

An armistice is an agreement between opposing military forces to stop shooting at each other. Initiated by field commanders, it is not a treaty, nor does it officially bring an end to hostilities. In the case of the First World War, the conflict would conclude only in 1919 at Versailles, when the governments involved negotiated formal treaties of peace.

After seeing 1.4 million of his countrymen die in battle, a battle for which he believed Germany was responsible, Ferdinand Foch was in no mood to negotiate. Meeting in a railroad car in the woods near Compiegne, the Supreme Commander dictated the terms of the armistice to the German representatives. Not surprisingly, they were severe. In effect, they amounted to a surrender on the part of Germany.

The terms Foch set forth at Compiegne mandated:

• *the withdrawal of all German troops from France and Belgium*
• *the return of Alsace and Lorraine to France*
• *the transfer to the Allies of large amounts of military equipment*
• *the internment of the German navy in British ports*
• *the absence of German forces in German lands west of the Rhine*
• *the repudiation of the Treaty of Brest-Litovsk and*
• *reparations to make good Allied losses*

The emissaries had no choice but to accept. Early in the morning of November 11, having first checked with Prince Max and Hindenburg, Germany's representatives signed the document. The armistice was to take effect later that morning. The day before, the Kaiser had left for the Netherlands.

And so, at the eleventh hour on the eleventh day, of the eleventh month, the guns fell silent. The killing stopped and the blood battles of the Great War were consigned to history.

Around the world, but especially in Europe, people prayed that never again would such a conflict take place.

SELECTED QUESTIONS & ANSWERS

WHAT CAUSED THE FIRST WORLD WAR?

Clearly, the assassination of the Austrian archduke in June 1914 did not cause the war. It simply set in motion a sequence of events that, given the failure of diplomacy, resulted in European nations declaring war upon one another.

The actual causes of the Great War are complex, multiple, and interrelated. They included economic competition and African colonialism, naval ambitions and military alliances, plus extreme national pride and historical animosities. Add to this explosive mix ignorance and fear and the consequences become deadly.

Yet, despite this volatility, it is worth noting that Great Britain did not strike the first blow. Nor did France, however anxious the latter was to recover Alsace and Lorraine. Moreover, Austrian-Hungary's decision to invade Serbia need not have produced a wider conflict since most European leaders accepted the Hapsburg's need to respond to Franz Ferdinand's murder. There had been prior localized Balkan wars and one more need not have caused Europe to erupt. That left Russia and Germany, two nations with little love for one another. Historians see Russia's decision to mobilize its military as a decisive step. Once the Tsar called up his army, Germany went to war.

In 1914, Germany was a rising industrial power, eager to

gain a larger and more respected role in the world. It also was
a nation in which the army wielded considerable political influence. The Germany of Kaiser Wilhelm II was a nation
comfortable with the idea of war, which it viewed as an appropriate means by which to conduct foreign policy. To most
Germans, Russia constituted a threat to German culture and
the country's economic prosperity. So, when the Tsar called
up his troops, Germany took action. Germany alone did not
cause the First World War, but its troops were the first to strike.

HOW MANY MEN DIED IN BATTLE DURING THE FIRST WORLD WAR?

World War One was an extremely bloody affair. Battle
deaths, by nation (excluding the United States), are shown
below. The list is taken from one of the better books on the
conflict, H.P. Willmott's *World War One*.[28] Other authors cite
similar, though not identical, numbers.

> *Russia - 1,800,000*
> *France - 1,390,000*
> *British Empire - 900,000*
> *Italy - 460,000*
> *Germany - 2,040,000*
> *Austria-Hungary - 1,020,000*
> *Turkey - 240,000*
> *Bulgaria - 80,000*

These numbers total 7,930,000. Add to this total the number of deaths sustained by Serbia and Romania and the
number exceeds eight million. Even this figure may be low.
Civilian deaths also were high. At least seven million non-mil-
itary men and women lost their lives as a result of the war.

Casualty figures for the Unites States reflect its army's late
arrival in France and its limited combat role. American battle
deaths number 50,280.[29] Fifty thousand dead soldiers is not

an insignificant loss. Today, eight U.S. military cemeteries in Europe attest to the sacrifice made by the American Expeditionary Force. Yet, relative to the losses sustained by other nations, the number is quite small.

Pershing's army also had some 205,000 men wounded. This number too is small in comparison to what Britain, Germany, and the others sustained. France, for example, saw 4.3 million of its soldiers in need of medical attention.

Perhaps surprisingly, the First World War was not the most deadly event of the early twentieth century. That dubious distinction belongs to the flu pandemic that struck in 1918 and 1919. Worldwide, the flu took the lives of 21 million people and possibly more.

WHY DID SO MANY MEN DIE IN THE FIRST WORLD WAR?

The war was a bloodbath because two weapons widely employed were particularly lethal. The machine gun and the cannon were extremely effective at killing soldiers. Machine guns cut down waves of advancing men while artillery fire, delivered in vast quantities, became highly accurate. It was the latter that caused the greatest loss of life. In his memoirs, written in Sweden shortly after the war, Hindenburg writes that his army's most dangerous opponent was French artillery.[30]

Another reason why so many men died in the First World War was that the tactics employed by generals such as Haig and Pershing were flawed. Having soldiers attack machine guns head on or having infantry walk line abreast across open fields were recipes for disaster. Yet, both commanders, and other generals as well, did just that.

WAS FIELD MARSHAL SIR DOUGLAS HAIG AN INCOMPETENT COMMANDER?

History has not been kind to Sir Douglas. Although his army was victorious and he won several battles, Haig is seen as the archetypical inept general of World War One, insensitive to the loss of life, while remaining comfortable and safe far from the enemy lines. The image is only partially correct. True, he appeared unconcerned about the great losses his army sustained. And, he was not exposed to enemy fire (although several British generals were and paid with their lives) nor were his tactics in 1916 and 1917 the best. But commanding generals are not supposed to be on the front line. Their job is to prepare for and manage the battle, and that can be done only in the rear. No one in 1915-1917 knew how to break through tiered layers of defense or, if they knew—and later on some did—the resources available were not up to the task. By 1918, however, Haig's armies employed tactics that enabled British troops to crack German defenses. Massive artillery fire, tanks, and infantry, all coordinated, were the formula for success. When, in September 1918, the British army swept through the Hindenburg Line, Haig and his staff demonstrated they knew how to wage war.

Still, the carnage of the Somme and of Passchendaele lingers, and will be linked forever with the name of Douglas Haig.

WHY WERE PARACHUTES NOT WIDELY USED?

Parachutes were available in 1914 and could have been employed throughout the war. The fact that they were not today seems foolish. Parachutes, however, were issued to balloon crews and, toward the very end of the conflict, to German pilots. But French, American and British aviators did not have them. At first, the reason was one of weight. Early warplanes were light and utilized engines that were underpowered. The additional weight of a packed parachute adversely affected aircraft performance. But as planes grew more robust a parachute's weight mattered little. Still, the pilots of SPADS, Camels and Fokker Triplanes were not issued this simple piece of lifesaving equipment. Why? Apparently, because commanders believed that with such a device available, pilots and observers would readily abandon the plane. Knowing there was no easy exit, pilots, particularly pursuit pilots, would stay in the fight and give it their all.

WERE THE TERMS OF THE ARMISTICE TOO LENIENT?

By November 1918, the German army was a spent force. Ludendorff and Hindenburg understood that victory was not possible, and that Germany needed to sue for peace. At Compiegne, the terms Foch set forth in the armistice amounted to surrender on the part of the German military. But Germany never formally surrendered. No surrender ceremony took place; no such document was signed. German soldiers simply turned around and marched home. In Berlin, a victory parade was held, but its participants were German. British, French, and American troops made no celebratory march through Germany's towns and cities.

This was a mistake. In the years following the war, German citizens and former soldiers were able to convince themselves that, as the army had not surrendered, Germany's defeat must have been brought about not by its armed services, but by forces at home. They blamed left-wing radicals, war profiteers, and the Jews. The Fatherland, they agreed, had been stabbed in the back. This contention, false though it was, gained credence in postwar Germany. Among its proponents was a former corporal in the Kaiser's army by the name of Adolph Hitler.

Should the Allies have continued to fight past November 11, forcing Germany to surrender? Haig thought not. Why? Because the British army would have to do most of the fighting.[31] Foch saw the armistice as entirely sufficient. At Compiegne, the French had gotten what they wanted, the return of Alsace and Lorraine, etc., without the need for further bloodshed. Only Pershing disagreed. He thought the armistice

premature.[32] Black Jack wanted the troops Foch commanded
to destroy the German army, thus making clear to everyone
that the Allies had won and that Germany had lost. Otherwise,
he believed, another war might have to be fought.

WHY DID THE UNITED STATES NOT JOIN THE BATTLE EARLIER?

The U.S. declared war on Germany in April 1917, 31
months after the conflict started. In 1914, most Americans believed that Europe constantly went to war and that nothing
was to be gained by participating in a war that affected only
Europe. Americans would mind their own business and let the
French, British, and Germans go about killing themselves.
What changed their minds? British propaganda, the type of
submarine warfare the Germans resorted to in 1917, and
Wilson's desire to influence the postwar world resulted in the
U.S. change of heart. That American finances were tied to the
success of Britain and France, to whom they had extended sig-
nificant war credits (loans), was another contributing factor.

HOW EFFECTIVE WAS THE AMERICAN EXPEDITIONARY FORCE?

During World War One, American soldiers fought hard
and with great courage. Yet Pershing's army was inexperienced
and for this inexperience it paid a price, just as the British army
had early in the war. Writing in October 1918, as the Americans were battling in the Meuse-Argonne, Great Britain's most
senior field commander, Field Marshal Sir Douglas Haig,
described the AEF as "ill-equipped, half-trained, with insufficient supply services."[33]

Rarely does a novice army perform well in its early engagements. Combat is a learning experience and, in 1917, the
American Expeditionary Force had much to learn. In his
memoirs, Hindenburg wrote of the importance of experience,

saying that the losses sustained by the AEF "taught the United States for the future that the business of war cannot be learned in a few months, and that in a crisis lack of experience costs streams of blood."[34]

Pershing and his men struggled to master the art of war. Mistakes were made, yet not once were the Americans defeated in battle. There is little doubt that, had the war continued into 1919, lessons would have been learned and the AEF would have become a most formidable fighting force.

WAS THE UNITED STATES ALONE RESPONSIBLE FOR THE ALLIED VICTORY IN WORLD WAR ONE?

No, it was not. America played a part in the war's outcome, a significant part, but the United States did not cause the defeat of Germany and its partners.

As Captain B.H. Liddell Hart has written, no single factor can account for the victory of November 1918.[35] However, several factors can be seen as critical. One of these was Britain's naval blockade. This ruined the Germany economy and weakened the Kaiser's army. Another was the grit shown by the French army, which, despite setbacks, continued the fight from the first day of the war to the last. Still another, not mentioned by Liddell Hart, was that Germany took on not only France and Russia, but also Great Britain and the United States. In doing so, Germany was simply outmatched.

Most certainly, Americans contributed to Germany's defeat. In battle, the AEF engaged the German army and helped to grind it down. But America's more important contribution was to lift the spirits of the French and British, both at home and on the battlefield. American involvement made them believe victory was possible. The British and French had been fighting hard since 1914 and, after sustaining horrendous losses, were no longer convinced Germany would be beaten. Enter the United States. In 1917 and 1918, America sent to Europe

thousands and thousands of healthy young men eager to fight.
Commented Liddell Hart:

> *The United States did not win the war, but without their eco-*
> *nomic aid to ease the strain, without the arrival of their troops*
> *to turn the numerical balance, and, above all, without the moral*
> *tonic which their coming gave, victory would have been impos-*
> *sible.*[36]

SELECTED READINGS

Bowen, Ezra, *Knights of the Air*, Time-Life Books, Alexandria, 1980.

Carver, Field Marshal Sir Michael, Editor, *The War Lords: Military Commanders of the Twentieth Century*, Little, Brown and Company, Boston, 1976.

Farwell, Byron, *Over There: The United States in the Great War 1917-1918*, W.W. Norton and Company, New York, 1999.

Franks, Norman, *American Aces of World War I*, Osprey, Oxford, 2001.

Hindenburg, Field Marshal von, *The Great War*, Edited by Charles Messenger, Greenhill Books, London, 2006.

Hough, Richard, *The Great War at Sea 1914-1918*, Oxford University Press, 1983.

Keegan, John, *The First World War*, Alfred A. Knopf, New York, 1999.

Lengel, Edward G., *To Conquer Hell: The Meuse-Argonne, 1918*, Henry Holt and Company, New York, 2008.

Liddell Hart, Captain B. H., *The Real War 1914-1918*, Little, Brown and Company, Boston, 1930.

Neiberg, Michael S., *Fighting the Great War: A Global History*, Harvard University Press, Cambridge, 2005.

Prior, Robin and Wilson, Trevor, *The First World War*, Cassell, London, 1999.

Strachan, Hew, *The First World War*, Viking, New York, 2003.

Terraine, John, *Douglas Haig: The Educated Soldier*, Hutchison, London, 1963.

Votaw, John F., *The American Expeditionary Forces in World War I*, Osprey, London, 2005.

Willmott, H. P., *World War I*, DK Books, New York, 2003.

NOTES

[1] John Keegan, *The First World War*, Alfred A. Knopf, New York, 1999. p.119.

[2] Keegan, p. 133.

[3] Hew Strachan, *The First World War*, First American Edition, Viking, 2003. p. 31.

[4] John Terraine, *Douglas Haig: The Educated Soldier*, Hutchison, London, 1963. p. 231.

[5] Keegan, p. 299.

[6] Terraine, p. 232.

[7] Keegan, p. 355.

[8] Captain B. H. Liddell Hart, *The Real War 1914-1918*, Little Brown, Boston, 1930. p. 471.

[9] Richard Hough, *The Great War at Sea 1914-1918*, Oxford University Press, Oxford, 1983. p. 169.

[10] H. W. Brands, *Woodrow Wilson*, The American Presidents, Arthur M. Schlesinger, Jr., General Editor, Henry Holt and Company, New York, 2003. p. 80.

[11] Strachan, p. xvii and p. 227.

[12] Michael S. Neiberg, *Fighting the Great War: A Global History*, Harvard University Press, Cambridge, 2005. p. 327.

[13] John F. Votaw, *The American Expeditionary Force in World War I*, Osprey, Oxford, 2005. p. 32-34.

[14] Byron Farwell, *Over There: The United States in the Great War, 1917-1918*, W.W. Norton and Company, New York, 1999. p. 234.

[15] John Terraine, *The U-Boat Wars: 1916-1945*, G. P. Putnam and Sons, New York, 1989. p. 115.

[16] Terraine, *Douglas Haig*, p. 433-434.

[17] David Bonk, *Chateau-Thierry & Belleau Wood 1918: America's Baptism of Fire on the Marne*, Osprey, Oxford, 2007. p. 35.

[18] William R. Griffiths, *The Great War: Strategies and Tactics of the First World War*, Thomas E. Greiss, Series Editor, The West Point Military History Series, Square One, Garden City Park, 2003. p. 155.

[19] Keegan, p. 412.

[20] Farwell, p. 209.

[21] Ezra Bowen, *Knights of the Air*, The Epic of Flight Series, Time-Life Books, Alexandria, 1980. p. 82-83 and p. 175.

[22] Mark R. Henry, *The U. S. Army of World War I*, Men-at-Arms Series, Osprey, Oxford, 2003. p. 13.

[23] Keegan, p. 412, and Farwell, p. 218.

[24] Edward G. Lengel, *To Conquer Hell: The Meuse-Argonne, 1918*, Henry Holt and Company, New York, 2008. p. 381.

[25] Lengel, p. 420.

[26] Lengel, p. 385.

[27] H. P. Willmott, *World War I*, First American Edition, DK-Dorling Kindersley Publishing, New York, 2003. p. 266.

[28] Willmott, p. 307.

[29] Votaw, p. 41.

[30] Field Marshal von Hindenburg, *The Great War*, Edited by Charles Messenger, Greenhill Books, London, 2006. p. 166.

[31] Terraine, *Douglas Haig*, p. 476.

[32] Farwell, p. 257.

[33] Terraine, *Douglas Haig*, p. 476.

[34] von Hindenburg, p. 223.

[35] Liddell Hart, p. 476.

[36] Liddell Hart, p. 476.